Easy to Use

PICK UP & PLAY

UKULELE CHORDS

QUICK START, EASY DIAGRAMS

SEE IT ▓ HEAR IT

JAKE JACKSON

mobile
online
in print

Flame Tree
Music
BOOKS • eBOOKS • RESOURCES

Contents

Publisher/Creative Director: Nick Wells • Project Editor: Gillian Whitaker
Layout Design: Jane Ashley • Website and Software: David Neville
with Stevens Dumpala and Steve Moulton

First published 2019 by **FLAME TREE PUBLISHING**
6 Melbray Mews, Fulham, London SW6 3NS, United Kingdom
www.flametreepublishing.com

Music information site: www.flametreemusic.com

19 20 21 22 23 24 • 1 2 3 4 5 6 7 8 9 10

The CIP record for this book is available from the British Library.

ISBN: 978-1-78755-688-1

Jake Jackson is a writer and musician. He has created and contributed to over 25 practical music books, including *Guitar Chords* and *How to Play Guitar*. His music is available on iTunes, Amazon and Spotify amongst others.

Every effort has been made to contact copyright holders. We apologize in advance for any omissions and would be pleased to insert the appropriate acknowledgement in subsequent editions of this publication.

Android is a trademark of Google Inc. Logic Pro, iPhone and iPad are either registered trademarks or trademarks of Apple Computer Inc. in the United States and/or other countries. Cubase is a registered trademark or trademark of Steinberg Media Technologies GmbH, a wholly owned subsidiary of Yamaha Corporation, in the United States and/or other countries. Nokia's product names are either trademarks or registered trademarks of Nokia. Nokia is a registered trademark of Nokia Corporation in the United States and/or other countries. Samsung and Galaxy S are both registered trademarks of Samsung Electronics America, Ltd. in the United States and/or other countries.

Printed in China

Ukulele Chords
An Introduction

Learning to play the ukulele can be fun and rewarding. Whether playing on your own, with friends, or listening and playing along to songs, the ukulele is a great instrument to pick up and play.

The quickest way to start is to learn some chords. They are the building blocks of all musical compositions so we've tried to make the following pages as straightforward as possible, so you can start to play straightaway. The book is organized by key and offers you plenty of information to help you build your understanding. Each chord is clearly laid out, giving you the musical spelling, and the notes on each string of the instrument.

For the ukulele there are two main techniques for the right hand: finger picking and strumming. A simple right hand movement would be:

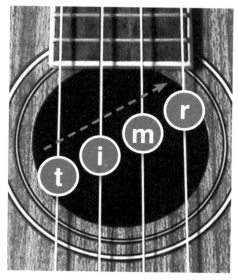

thumb   index   middle   ring

The Diagrams
A Quick Guide

Each step on the fretboard represents a note. Each note up the fretboard is higher than the one it precedes. The difference between each note is called an interval, and these intervals are used to make scales, which in turn are used to make chords.

About the Notes

Playing every note on a piano, from left to right, using all the white and the black keys, is similar to playing every note on every string from bass to treble strings on a guitar.

A standard ukulele is different because although every fret represents a different interval, the standard tuning of most ukuleles presents a G string that is only two intervals lower than the top, A string. This gives the ukulele its unique high-pitched tone and means that the **root note** of a chord (i.e. the note that gives the chord its name) is **often on the 3rd string**.

4

Chord Name

Each chord is given a short and complete name, for example the short name **Cm** is properly known as C minor.

Left Hand Fingerings

1 is the index finger
2 is the middle finger
3 is the ring finger
4 is the little finger

Tuning the Ukulele

The **open strings** on a ukulele work in a different way to a guitar: the bottom string is just two notes lower than the top.

This gives the characteristic jangling sound. See below for the same notes on a piano. **Middle C** is shown in red.

G   C   E   A

C   E   G   A

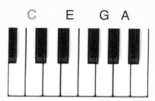

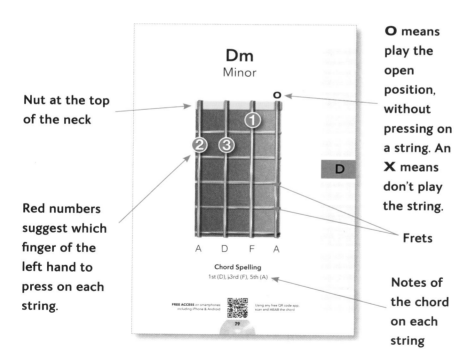

Nut at the top of the neck

Red numbers suggest which finger of the left hand to press on each string.

O means play the open position, without pressing on a string. An **X** means don't play the string.

Frets

Notes of the chord on each string

Dm
Minor

A   D   F   A

Chord Spelling
1st (D), ♭3rd (F), 5th (A)

FREE ACCESS on smartphones
including iPhone & Android

Using any free QR code app,
scan and HEAR the chord

79

The Sound Links
Another Quick Guide

Requirements: a camera and internet-ready smartphone (e.g. **iPhone**, any **Android** phone (e.g. **Samsung Galaxy**), **Nokia Lumia**, or **camera-enabled tablet** such as the **iPad Mini**). The best result is achieved using a WIFI connection.

1. Try to read the QR codes with your phone's camera. This should open the link. Failing that, download any **free QR code reader**. An app store search will reveal a great many of these, so don't be afraid to try a few before you settle on the one that works best for you. Tapmedia's QR Reader app is good, or ATT Scanner (used below) or QR Media. Some of the free apps have ads, which can be annoying.

2. On your smartphone, open the app and **scan** the **QR code** at the base of any particular page.

FREE ACCESS on smartphones including iPhone & Android

Using any free QR code app, scan and HEAR the chord

79

3. Scanning the chord will bring you to the C major chord, and from there you can access and hear the complete library of scales and chords on flametreemusic.com.

FREE ACCESS on smartphones including iPhone & Android

Using any free QR code app, scan and HEAR the chord

In the chord section, the QR code at the bottom of those pages will take you directly to the relevant chord on the website.

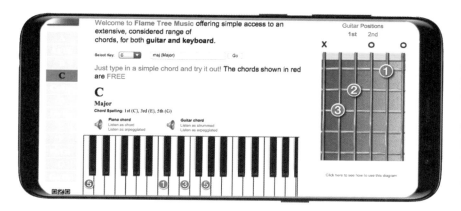

4. Use the menu to choose from **20 scales** or 12 **free chords** per key.

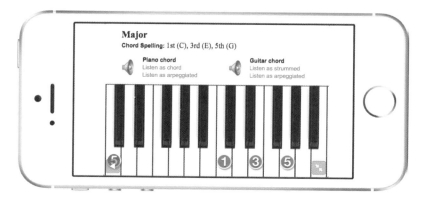

5. Click the sounds! Both piano and guitar audio is provided. This is particularly helpful when you're playing with others.

The QR codes give you direct access to chords and scales. You can access a much wider range of chords if you register and subscribe.

FREE ACCESS on smartphones including iPhone & Android

Using any free QR code app, scan and **HEAR** the chord

A
Major

A   C♯   E   A

Chord Spelling
1st (A), 3rd (C♯), 5th (E)

Am
Minor

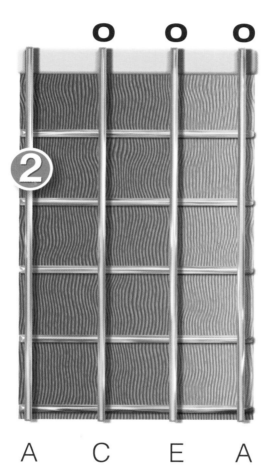

A   C   E   A

Chord Spelling
1st (A), ♭3rd (C), 5th (E)

A+
Augmented Triad

A   C♯   E♯   A

Chord Spelling
1st (A), 3rd (C♯), ♯5th (E♯)

FREE ACCESS on smartphones including iPhone & Android

Using any free QR code app, scan and **HEAR** the chord

A°
Diminished Triad

A   E♭   C

Chord Spelling
1st (A), ♭3rd (C), ♭5th (E♭)

Asus2
Suspended 2nd

A   E   E   B

Chord Spelling
1st (A), 2nd (B), 5th (E)

FREE ACCESS on smartphones
including iPhone & Android

Using any free QR code app,
scan and **HEAR** the chord

A

A#/B♭

B

C

C#/D♭

D

D#/E♭

E

F

F#/G♭

G

G#/A♭

Asus4
Suspended 4th

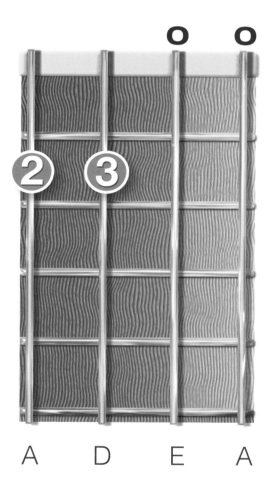

A   D   E   A

Chord Spelling
1st (A), 4th (D), 5th (E)

A6
Major 6th

A   E   F#   C#

Chord Spelling
1st (A), 3rd (C#), 5th (E), 6th (F#)

FREE ACCESS on smartphones
including iPhone & Android

Using any free QR code app,
scan and **HEAR** the chord

Am6
Minor 6th

A   E   F#   C

Chord Spelling
1st (A), ♭3rd (C), 5th (E), 6th (F#)

Amaj7
Major 7th

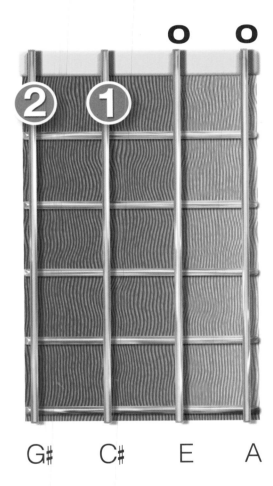

G#   C#   E   A

Chord Spelling
1st (A), 3rd (C#), 5th (E), 7th (G#)

A7
Dominant 7th

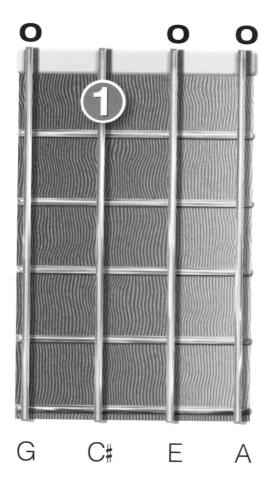

G   C#   E   A

Chord Spelling
1st (A), 3rd (C#), 5th (E), ♭7th (G)

17

A7sus4
Dominant 7th
Suspended 4th

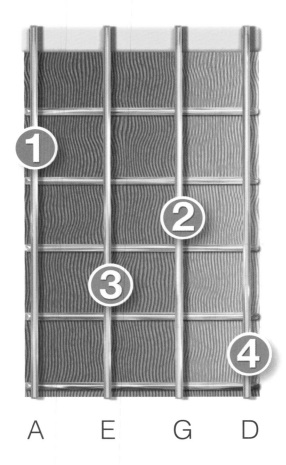

A   E   G   D

Chord Spelling
1st (A), 4th (D), 5th (E), ♭7th (G)

Am7
Minor 7th

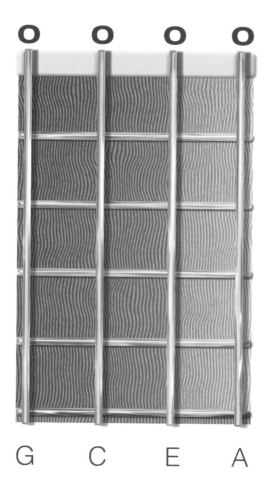

G   C   E   A

Chord Spelling
1st (A), ♭3rd (C), 5th (E), ♭7th (G)

Using any free QR code app,
scan and **HEAR** the chord

A°7
Diminished 7th

A   E♭   G♭   C

Chord Spelling
1st (A), ♭3rd (C), ♭5th (E♭), ♭♭7th (G♭)

Aadd9
Major add 9th

O

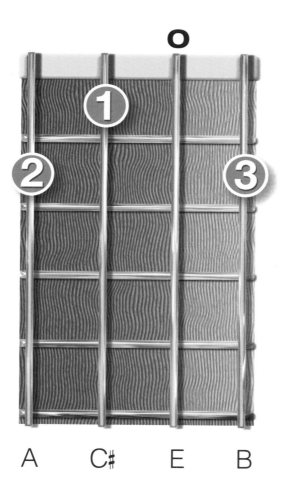

A   C#   E   B

Chord Spelling
1st (A), 3rd (C#), 5th (E), 9th (B)

FREE ACCESS on smartphones
including iPhone & Android

Using any free QR code app,
scan and **HEAR** the chord

A♯/B♭
Major

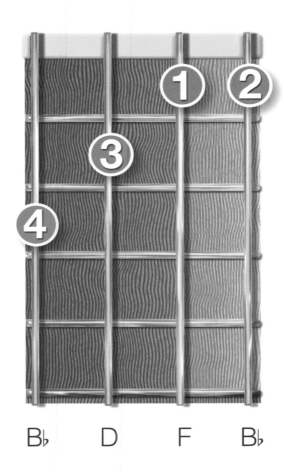

B♭   D   F   B♭

Chord Spelling
1st (B♭), 3rd (D), 5th (F)

A♯/B♭m
Minor

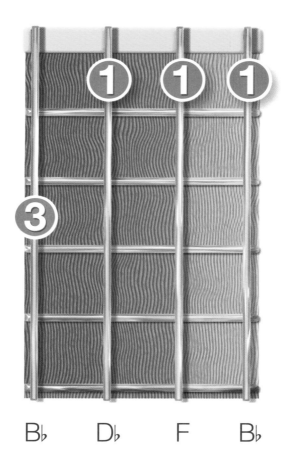

B♭   D♭   F   B♭

Chord Spelling
1st (B♭), ♭3rd (D♭), 5th (F)

FREE ACCESS on smartphones
including iPhone & Android

Using any free QR code app,
scan and **HEAR** the chord

23

A♯/B♭+
Augmented Triad

B♭   D   F♯   B♭

Chord Spelling
1st (B♭), 3rd (D), ♯5th (F♯)

A#/Bb°
Diminished Triad

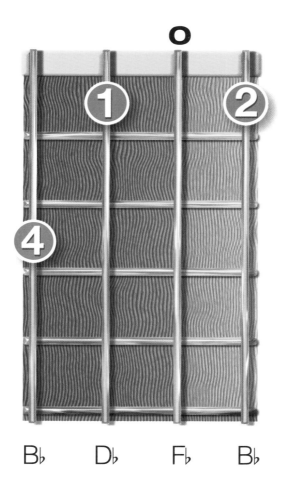

Bb   Db   Fb   Bb

Chord Spelling
1st (Bb), b3rd (Db), b5th (Fb)

FREE ACCESS on smartphones
including iPhone & Android

Using any free QR code app,
scan and **HEAR** the chord

A#/B♭sus2
Suspended 2nd

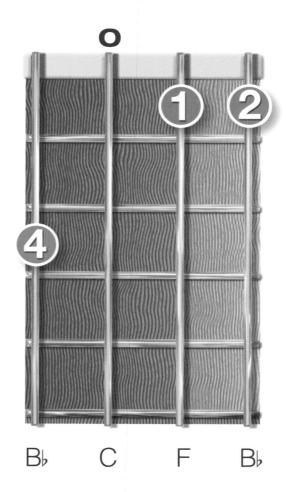

O

Bb   C   F   Bb

Chord Spelling
1st (B♭), 2nd (C), 5th (F)

A♯/B♭sus4
Suspended 4th

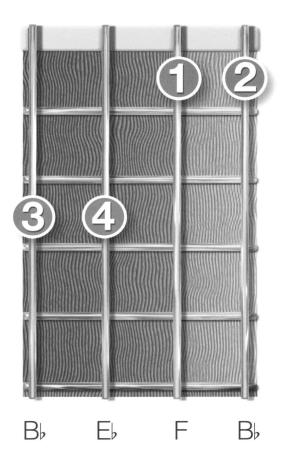

B♭   E♭   F   B♭

Chord Spelling
1st (B♭), 4th (E♭), 5th (F)

A#/B♭6
Major 6th

O

G   D   F   B♭

Chord Spelling
1st (B♭), 3rd (D), 5th (F), 6th (G)

A♯/B♭m6
Minor 6th

G   D♭   F   B♭

Chord Spelling
1st (B♭), ♭3rd (D♭), 5th (F), 6th (G)

FREE ACCESS on smartphones
including iPhone & Android

Using any free QR code app,
scan and **HEAR** the chord

29

A♯/B♭maj7
Major 7th

A   D   F   B♭

Chord Spelling
1st (B♭), 3rd (D), 5th (F), 7th (A)

A♯/B♭7
Dominant 7th

A♭   D   F   B♭

Chord Spelling
1st (B♭), 3rd (D), 5th (F), ♭7th (A♭)

FREE ACCESS on smartphones
including iPhone & Android

Using any free QR code app,
scan and **HEAR** the chord

A#/B♭7sus4
Dominant 7th
Suspended 4th

A♭   E♭   F   B♭

Chord Spelling
1st (B♭), 4th (E♭), 5th (F), ♭7th (A♭)

A#/B♭m7
Minor 7th

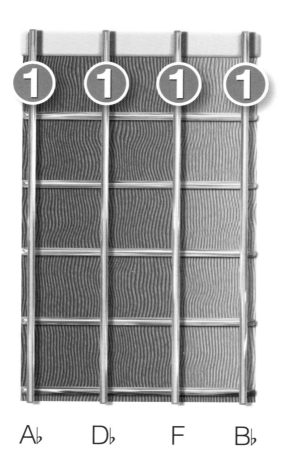

A♭   D♭   F   B♭

Chord Spelling
1st (B♭), ♭3rd (D♭), 5th (F), ♭7th (A♭)

FREE ACCESS on smartphones
including iPhone & Android

Using any free QR code app,
scan and **HEAR** the chord

A#/B♭°7
Diminished 7th

A𝄫 D♭ F♭ B♭

Chord Spelling

1st (B♭), ♭3rd (D♭), ♭5th (F♭), 𝄫7th (A𝄫)

A♯/B♭add9
Major add 9th

Bb   D   F   C

Chord Spelling
1st (B♭), 3rd (D), 5th (F), 9th (C)

A♯/B♭

B
Major

B   D#   F#   B

Chord Spelling
1st (B), 3rd (D#), 5th (F#)

Bm
Minor

B   D   F#   B

Chord Spelling
1st (B), ♭3rd (D), 5th (F#)

Using any free QR code app, scan and **HEAR** the chord

B+
Augmented

B   D♯   F𝄪   B

Chord Spelling
1st (B), 3rd (D♯), ♯5th (F𝄪)

B°
Diminished

B   D   F   B

Chord Spelling
1st (B), ♭3rd (D), ♭5th (F)

Bsus2
Suspended 2nd

B   C#   F#   B

Chord Spelling
1st (B), 2nd (C#), 5th (F#)

Bsus4
Suspended 4th

B E F♯ B

Chord Spelling
1st (B), 4th (E), 5th (F♯)

B6
Major 6th

G# D# F# B

Chord Spelling
1st (B), 3rd (D#), 5th (F#), 6th (G#)

A
A#/Bb
B
C
C#/Db
D
D#/Eb
E
F
F#/Gb
G
G#/Ab

Bm6
Minor 6th

G#   D   F#   B

Chord Spelling
1st (B), b3rd (D), 5th (F#), 6th (G#)

Bmaj7
Major 7th

A
A#/Bb
B
C
C#/Db
D
D#/Eb
E
F
F#/Gb
G
G#/Ab

A#   D#   F#   B

Chord Spelling
1st (B), 3rd (D#), 5th (F#), 7th (A#)

FREE ACCESS on smartphones
including iPhone & Android

Using any free QR code app,
scan and **HEAR** the chord

B7
Dominant 7th

A   D#   F#   B

Chord Spelling
1st (B), 3rd (D#), 5th (F#), ♭7th (A)

FREE ACCESS on smartphones
including iPhone & Android

Using any free QR code app,
scan and **HEAR** the chord

B7sus4
Dominant 7th
Suspended 4th

A   E   F♯   B

Chord Spelling
1st (B), 4th (E), 5th (F♯), ♭7th (A)

Bm7
Minor 7th

A   D   F♯   B

Chord Spelling
1st (B), ♭3rd (D), 5th (F♯), ♭7th (A)

FREE ACCESS on smartphones
including iPhone & Android

Using any free QR code app,
scan and **HEAR** the chord

B°7
Diminished 7th

A♭   D   F   B

Chord Spelling
1st (B), ♭3rd (D), ♭5th (F), ♭♭7th (A♭)

FREE ACCESS on smartphones
including iPhone & Android

Using any free QR code app,
scan and **HEAR** the chord

48

Badd9
Major add 9th

B   D#   F#   C#

Chord Spelling
1st (B), 3rd (D#), 5th (F#), 9th (C#)

C
Major

O   O   O

③

G   C   E   C

Chord Spelling
1st (C), 3rd (E), 5th (G)

Cm
Minor

O

G   E♭   G   C

Chord Spelling
1st (C), ♭3rd (E♭), 5th (G)

C

C+
Augmented Triad

G♯   C   E   C

Chord Spelling
1st (C), 3rd (E), ♯5th (G♯)

C°
Diminished Triad

X

① ② ③

E♭   G♭   C

Chord Spelling
1st (C), ♭3rd (E♭), ♭5th (G♭)

A

A#/B♭

B

C

C#/D♭

D

D#/E♭

E

F

F#/G♭

G

G#/A♭

Csus2
Suspended 2nd

O

G   D   G   C

Chord Spelling
1st (C), 2nd (D), 5th (G)

Csus4
Suspended 4th

G   C   F   C

C

Chord Spelling
1st (C), 4th (F), 5th (G)

C6
Major 6th

G   C   E   A

Chord Spelling
1st (C), 3rd (E), 5th (G), 6th (A)

Cm6
Minor 6th

O

G   E♭   A   C

Chord Spelling
1st (C), ♭3rd (E♭), 5th (G), 6th (A)

C

Cmaj7
Major 7th

G C E B

Chord Spelling
1st (C), 3rd (E), 5th (G), 7th (B)

A
A#/Bb
B
C
C#/Db
D
D#/Eb
E
F
F#/Gb
G
G#/Ab

C7
Dominant 7th

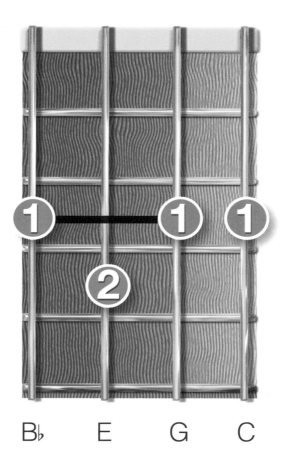

Bb   E   G   C

Chord Spelling
1st (C), 3rd (E), 5th (G), b7th (Bb)

C7sus4
Dominant 7th
Suspended 4th

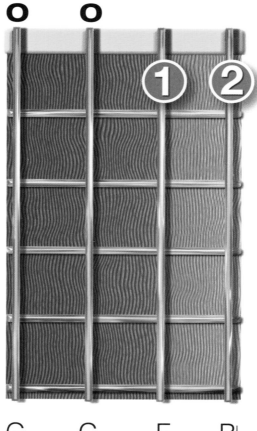

G   C   F   B♭

Chord Spelling
1st (C), 4th (F), 5th (G), ♭7th (B♭)

Cm7
Minor 7th

B♭   E♭   G   C

Chord Spelling
1st (C), ♭3rd (E♭), 5th (G), ♭7th (B♭)

FREE ACCESS on smartphones
including iPhone & Android

Using any free QR code app,
scan and **HEAR** the chord

C°7
Diminished 7th

B♭♭   E♭   G♭   C

Chord Spelling
1st (C), ♭3rd (E♭), ♭5th (G♭), ♭♭7th (B♭♭)

A

A♯/B♭

B

C

C♯/D♭

D

D♯/E♭

E

F

F♯/G♭

G

G♯/A♭

Cadd9
Major add 9th

O   O

G   D   E   C

C

Chord Spelling
1st (C), 3rd (E), 5th (G), 9th (D)

C#/Db
Major

G#   C#   E#   C#

Chord Spelling
1st (C#), 3rd (E#), 5th (G#)

C#/D♭m
Minor

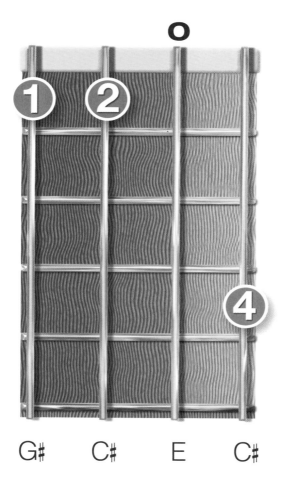

o

1 **2** **4**

G#   C#   E   C#

Chord Spelling
1st (C#), ♭3rd (E), 5th (G#)

C#/D♭

C♯/D♭+
Augmented Triad

Gⅹ   C♯   E♯   C♯

Chord Spelling
1st (C♯), 3rd (E♯), ♯5th (Gⅹ)

C#/Db°
Diminished Triad

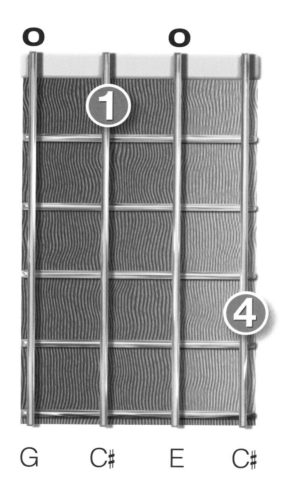

G   C#   E   C#

Chord Spelling
1st (C#), b3rd (E), b5th (G)

FREE ACCESS on smartphones
including iPhone & Android

Using any free QR code app,
scan and **HEAR** the chord

C#/D♭sus2
Suspended 2nd

A

A#/B♭

B

C

C#/D♭

D

D#/E♭

E

F

F#/G♭

G

G#/A♭

G#   D#   G#   C#

Chord Spelling
1st (C#), 2nd (D#), 5th (G#)

FREE ACCESS on smartphones
including iPhone & Android

Using any free QR code app,
scan and **HEAR** the chord

68

C♯/D♭sus4
Suspended 4th

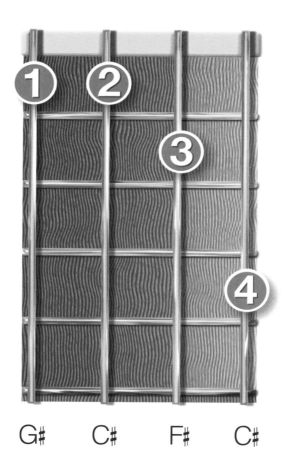

G♯   C♯   F♯   C♯

Chord Spelling
1st (C♯), 4th (F♯), 5th (G♯)

FREE ACCESS on smartphones
including iPhone & Android

Using any free QR code app,
scan and **HEAR** the chord

C#/D♭6
Major 6th

G#   C#   E#   A#

Chord Spelling
1st (C#), 3rd (E#), 5th (G#), 6th (A#)

C♯/D♭m6

Minor 6th

C♯/D♭

G♯　　C♯　　E　　A♯

Chord Spelling

1st (C♯), ♭3rd (E), 5th (G♯), 6th (A♯)

C#/D♭maj7
Major 7th

G#   C#   E#   B#

Chord Spelling
1st (C#), 3rd (E#), 5th (G#), 7th (B#)

C#/D♭

A
A#/B♭
B
C
C#/D♭
D
D#/E♭
E
F
F#/G♭
G
G#/A♭

C♯/D♭7

Dominant 7th

G♯   C♯   E♯   B

Chord Spelling
1st (C♯), 3rd (E♯), 5th (G♯), ♭7th (B)

C#7sus4
Dominant 7th
Suspended 4th

G#   C#   F#   B

Chord Spelling
1st (C#), 4th (F#), 5th (G#), ♭7th (B)

FREE ACCESS on smartphones
including iPhone & Android

Using any free QR code app,
scan and **HEAR** the chord

C#/D♭m7
Minor 7th

G# C# E B

Chord Spelling
1st (C#), ♭3rd (E), 5th (G#), ♭7th (B)

C#/D♭

75

C#/D♭°7
Diminished 7th

G   C#   E   B♭

Chord Spelling
1st (C#), ♭3rd (E), ♭5th (G), ♭♭7th (B♭)

C♯/D♭add9
Major add 9th

G♯   D♯   E♯   C♯

Chord Spelling
1st (C♯), 3rd (E♯), 5th (G♯), 9th (D♯)

D
Major

o

② ③ ④

A   D   F#   A

Chord Spelling
1st (D), 3rd (F#), 5th (A)

A
A#/B♭
B
C
C#/D♭
D
D#/E♭
E
F
F#/G♭
G
G#/A♭

Dm
Minor

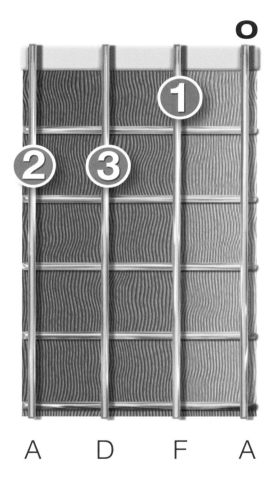

O

A   D   F   A

Chord Spelling
1st (D), ♭3rd (F), 5th (A)

D

D+
Augmented Triad

A#   D   F#   A#

Chord Spelling
1st (D), 3rd (F#), #5th (A#)

D°
Diminished Triad

A♭   D   F   D

D

Chord Spelling
1st (D), ♭3rd (F), ♭5th (A♭)

Dsus2
Suspended 2nd

A   D   E   A

Chord Spelling
1st (D), 2nd (E), 5th (A)

Dsus4
Suspended 4th

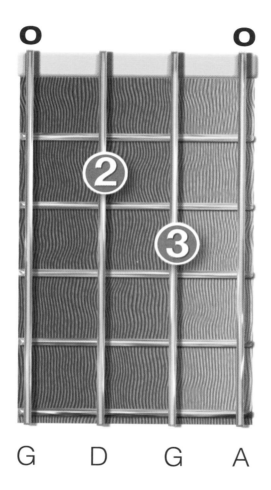

G   D   G   A

Chord Spelling
1st (D), 4th (G), 5th (A)

D

D6
Major 6th

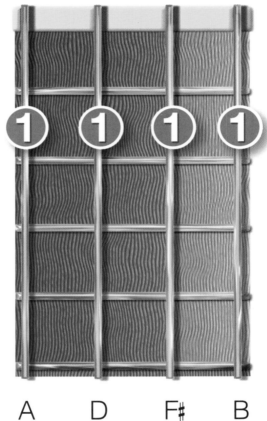

A   D   F#   B

Chord Spelling
1st (D), 3rd (F#), 5th (A), 6th (B)

A
A#/B♭
B
C
C#/D♭
D
D#/E♭
E
F
F#/G♭
G
G#/A♭

Dm6
Minor 6th

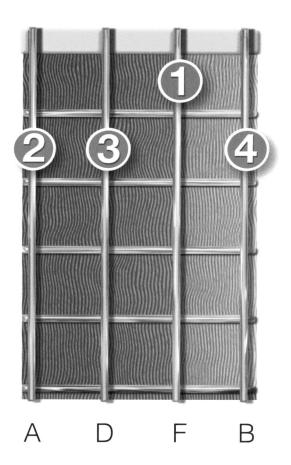

A   D   F   B

Chord Spelling
1st (D), ♭3rd (F), 5th (A), 6th (B)

Dmaj7
Major 7th

A   D   F#   C#

Chord Spelling
1st (D), 3rd (F#), 5th (A), 7th (C#)

A

A#/Bb

B

C

C#/Db

D

D#/Eb

E

F

F#/Gb

G

G#/Ab

D7
Dominant 7th

A   D   F♯   C

Chord Spelling
1st (D), 3rd (F♯), 5th (A), ♭7th (C)

D

D7sus4
Dominant 7th
Suspended 4th

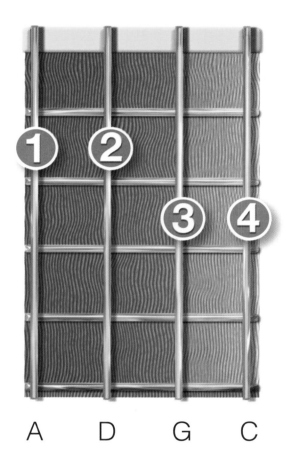

A   D   G   C

Chord Spelling
1st (D), 4th (G), 5th (A), ♭7th (C)

Dm7
Minor 7th

A   D   F   C

Chord Spelling
1st (D), ♭3rd (F), 5th (A), ♭7th (C)

D

D°7
Diminished 7th

A♭   D   F   C♭

Chord Spelling
1st (D), ♭3rd (F), ♭5th (A♭), ♭♭7th (C♭)

Dadd9
Major 9th

A E F♯ D

D

Chord Spelling
1st (D), 3rd (F♯), 5th (A), 9th (E)

D#/Eb
Major

O

① ③ ④

G   Eb   G   Bb

Chord Spelling
1st (Eb), 3rd (G), 5th (Bb)

A
A#/Bb
B
C
C#/Db
D
D#/Eb
E
F
F#/Gb
G
G#/Ab

D♯/E♭m
Minor

B♭   E♭   G♭   B♭

Chord Spelling
1st (E♭), ♭3rd (G♭), 5th (B♭)

D#/Eb+

Augmented Triad

O

G   Eb   G   B

Chord Spelling

1st (Eb), 3rd (G), #5th (B)

D♯/E♭°
Diminished Triad

O

② ③

④

B𝄫   E♭   G♭   B𝄫

Chord Spelling
1st (E♭), ♭3rd (G♭), ♭5th (B𝄫)

D♯/E♭

D♯/E♭sus2
Suspended 2nd

O

G   E♭   F   B♭

Chord Spelling
1st (E♭), 2nd (F), 5th (B♭)

D#/E♭sus4
Suspended 4th

B♭   E♭   A♭   B♭

D#/E♭

Chord Spelling
1st (E♭), 4th (A♭), 5th (B♭)

D#/E♭6
Major 6th

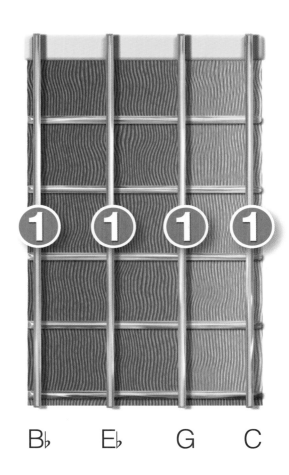

B♭   E♭   G   C

Chord Spelling
1st (E♭), 3rd (G), 5th (B♭), 6th (C)

D#/E♭m6

Minor 6th

B♭   E♭   G♭   C

Chord Spelling
1st (E♭), ♭3rd (G♭), 5th (B♭), 6th (C)

FREE ACCESS on smartphones
including iPhone & Android

Using any free QR code app,
scan and **HEAR** the chord

D♯/E♭maj7
Major 7th

| B♭ | E♭ | G | D |

Chord Spelling
1st (E♭), 3rd (G), 5th (B♭), 7th (D)

D♯/E♭7
Dominant 7th

B♭   E♭   G   D♭

Chord Spelling
1st (E♭), 3rd (G), 5th (B♭), ♭7th (D♭)

A

A♯/B♭

B

C

C♯/D♭

D

D♯/E♭

E

F

F♯/G♭

G

D#/Eb7sus4
Dominant 7th
Suspended 4th

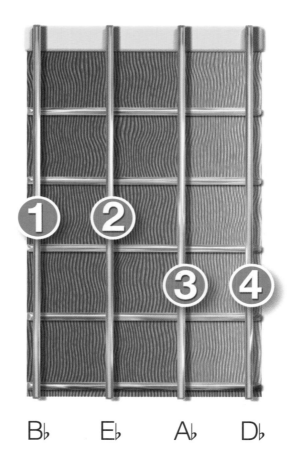

Bb   Eb   Ab   Db

Chord Spelling
1st (Eb), 4th (Ab), 5th (Bb), b7th (Db)

D#/E♭m7
Minor 7th

D#/E♭

B♭   E♭   G♭   D♭

Chord Spelling
1st (E♭), ♭3rd (G♭), 5th (B♭), ♭7th (D♭)

D♯/E♭°7
Diminished 7th

B𝄫   E♭   G♭   D𝄫

Chord Spelling
1st (E♭), ♭3rd (G♭), ♭5th (B𝄫), ♭♭7th (D𝄫)

D♯/E♭add9
Major add 9th

G   E♭   F   B♭

Chord Spelling
1st (E♭), 3rd (G), 5th (B♭), 9th (F)

E
Major

o

G#   E   E   B

Chord Spelling
1st (E), 3rd (G#), 5th (B)

Em
Minor

O

② ③ ④

G　E　G　B

Chord Spelling
1st (E), ♭3rd (G), 5th (B)

E

E+
Augmented Triad

G# E G# B#

Chord Spelling
1st (E), 3rd (G#), #5th (B#)

FREE ACCESS on smartphones including iPhone & Android

Using any free QR code app, scan and **HEAR** the chord

E°
Diminished Triad

O

① ③ ④

G   E   G   B♭

Chord Spelling
1st (E), ♭3rd (G), ♭5th (B♭)

E

Esus2
Suspended 2nd

B E F# B

Chord Spelling
1st (E), 2nd (F#), 5th (B)

Esus4
Suspended 4th

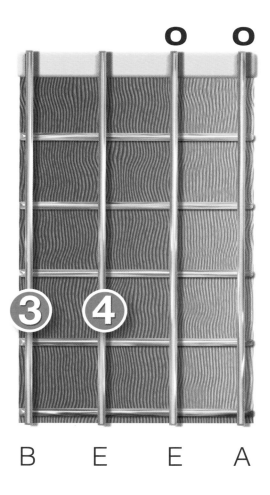

B   E   E   A

Chord Spelling
1st (E), 4th (A), 5th (B)

E

E6
Major 6th

G# C# E B

Chord Spelling
1st (E), 3rd (G#), 5th (B), 6th (C#)

FREE ACCESS on smartphones
including iPhone & Android

Using any free QR code app,
scan and **HEAR** the chord

Em6
Minor 6th

G   C#   E   B

Chord Spelling
1st (E), ♭3rd (G), 5th (B), 6th (C#)

E

Emaj7
Major 7th

O

① ② ③

G♯   D♯   E   B

Chord Spelling
1st (E), 3rd (G♯), 5th (B), 7th (D♯)

A
A♯/B♭
B
C
C♯/D♭
D
D♯/E♭
E
F
F♯/G♭
G
G♯/A♭

E7
Dominant 7th

O

G♯   D   E   B

Chord Spelling
1st (E), 3rd (G♯), 5th (B), ♭7th (D)

E

E7sus4
Dominant 7th
Suspended 4th

A   D   E   B

Chord Spelling
1st (E), 4th (A), 5th (B), ♭7th (D)

Em7
Minor 7th

G D E B

Chord Spelling
1st (E), ♭3rd (G), 5th (B), ♭7th (D)

A
A♯/B♭
B
C
C♯/D♭
D
D♯/E♭
E
F
F♯/G♭
G
G♯/A♭

E°7
Diminished 7th

G   D♭   E   B♭

Chord Spelling
1st (E), ♭3rd (G), ♭5th (B♭), ♭♭7th (D♭)

Eadd9
Major add 9th

G#   E   F#   B

Chord Spelling
1st (E), 3rd (G#), 5th (B), 9th (F#)

E

F
Major

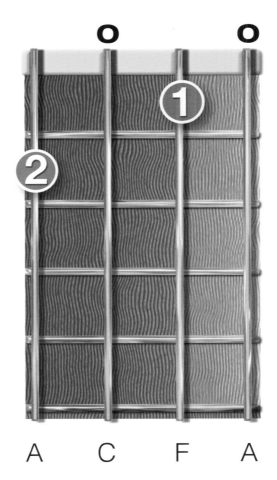

O   O

① ②

A   C   F   A

Chord Spelling
1st (F), 3rd (A), 5th (C)

A
A#/Bb
B
C
C#/Db
D
D#/Eb
E
F
F#/Gb
G
G#/Ab

Fm
Minor

| A♭ | C | F | C |

Chord Spelling
1st (F), ♭3rd (A♭), 5th (C)

F

F+
Augmented Triad

A   C#   F   A

Chord Spelling
1st (F), 3rd (A), #5th (C#)

FREE ACCESS on smartphones
including iPhone & Android

Using any free QR code app,
scan and **HEAR** the chord

F°
Diminished Triad

Cb   F   Ab   Cb

Chord Spelling
1st (F), ♭3rd (A♭), ♭5th (C♭)

F

Fsus2

Suspended 2nd

A
A#/Bb
B
C
C#/Db
D
D#/Eb
E
F
F#/Gb
G
G#/Ab

G   C   F   C

Chord Spelling
1st (F), 2nd (G), 5th (C)

FREE ACCESS on smartphones
including iPhone & Android

Using any free QR code app,
scan and **HEAR** the chord

Fsus4
Suspended 4th

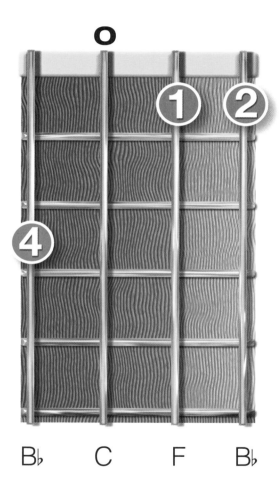

O

① ②

④

B♭   C   F   B♭

Chord Spelling
1st (F), 4th (B♭), 5th (C)

F

F6
Major 6th

A   D   F   C

Chord Spelling
1st (F), 3rd (A), 5th (C), 6th (D)

A
A#/Bb
B
C
C#/Db
D
D#/Eb
E
F
F#/Gb
G
G#/Ab

Fm6
Minor 6th

A♭   D   F   C

Chord Spelling
1st (F), ♭3rd (A♭), 5th (C), 6th (D)

F

Fmaj7
Major 7th

A   E   F   C

Chord Spelling
1st (F), 3rd (A), 5th (C), 7th (E)

A
A#/Bb
B
C
C#/Db
D
D#/Eb
E
F
F#/Gb
G
G#/Ab

F7
Dominant 7th

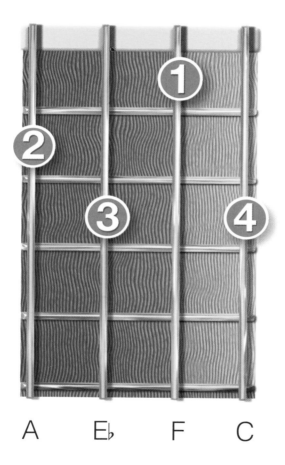

A   E♭   F   C

Chord Spelling
1st (F), 3rd (A), 5th (C), ♭7th (E♭)

F

F7sus4
Dominant 7th
Suspended 4th

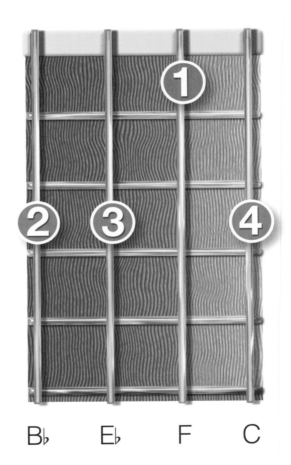

Bb   Eb   F   C

Chord Spelling
1st (F), 4th (Bb), 5th (C), b7th (Eb)

Fm7
Minor 7th

A♭   E♭   F   C

F

Chord Spelling
1st (F), ♭3rd (A♭), 5th (C), ♭7th (E♭)

FREE ACCESS on smartphones
including iPhone & Android

Using any free QR code app,
scan and **HEAR** the chord

131

F°7
Diminished 7th

Ab Ebb F Cb

Chord Spelling
1st (F), b3rd (Ab), b5th (Cb), bb7th (Ebb)

Fadd9
Major add 9th

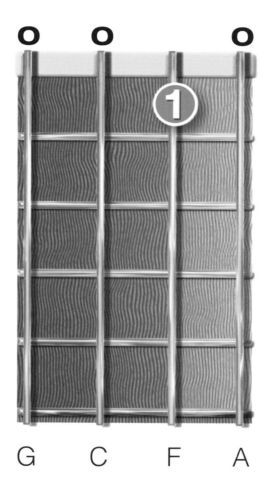

O   O   O

①

G   C   F   A

Chord Spelling
1st (F), 3rd (A), 5th (C), 9th (G)

F#/G♭
Major

A#   C#   F#   A#

Chord Spelling
1st (F#), 3rd (A#), 5th (C#)

FREE ACCESS on smartphones
including iPhone & Android

Using any free QR code app,
scan and **HEAR** the chord

F#/G♭m
Minor

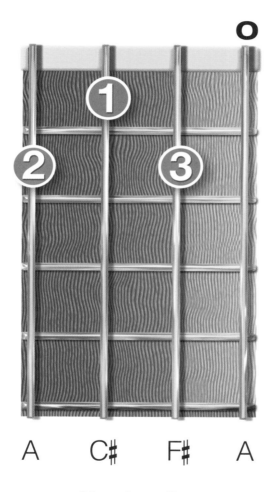

A   C#   F#   A

Chord Spelling
1st (F#), ♭3rd (A), 5th (C#)

F#/G♭

F♯/G♭+
Augmented Triad

A♯   C𝄪   F♯   A♯

Chord Spelling
1st (F♯), 3rd (A♯), ♯5th (C𝄪)

F♯/G♭°
Diminished Triad

A   C   F♯   A

Chord Spelling
1st (F♯), ♭3rd (A), ♭5th (C)

F♯/G♭

F#/G♭sus2
Suspended 2nd

G#   C#   F#   C#

Chord Spelling
1st (F#), 2nd (G#), 5th (C#)

A
A#/B♭
B
C
C#/D♭
D
D#/E♭
E
F
F#/G♭
G
G#/A♭

F♯/G♭sus4
Suspended 4th

B   C♯   F♯   B

Chord Spelling
1st (F♯), 4th (B), 5th (C♯)

F♯/G♭

F♯/G♭6
Major 6th

A♯   D♯   F♯   C♯

Chord Spelling
1st (F♯), 3rd (A♯), 5th (C♯), 6th (D♯)

FREE ACCESS on smartphones
including iPhone & Android

Using any free QR code app,
scan and **HEAR** the chord

F♯/G♭m6
Minor 6th

A D♯ F♯ C♯

F♯/G♭

Chord Spelling
1st (F♯), ♭3rd (A), 5th (C♯), 6th (D♯)

F#/G♭maj7
Major 7th

A#   E#   F#   C#

Chord Spelling
1st (F#), 3rd (A#), 5th (C#), 7th (E#)

A

A#/B♭

B

C

C#/D♭

D

D#/E♭

E

F

F#/G♭

G

G#/A♭

F#/G♭7

Dominant 7th

A#   E   F#   C#

Chord Spelling
1st (F#), 3rd (A#), 5th (C#), ♭7th (E)

F#/G♭

F#/Gb7sus4
Dominant 7th
Suspended 4th

B   E   F#   C#

Chord Spelling
1st (F#), 4th (B), 5th (C#), b7th (E)

F♯/G♭m7
Minor 7th

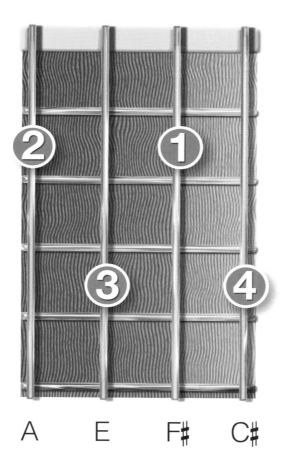

A   E   F♯   C♯

Chord Spelling
1st (F♯), ♭3rd (A), 5th (C♯), ♭7th (E)

F♯/G♭

F#/Gb°7
Diminished 7th

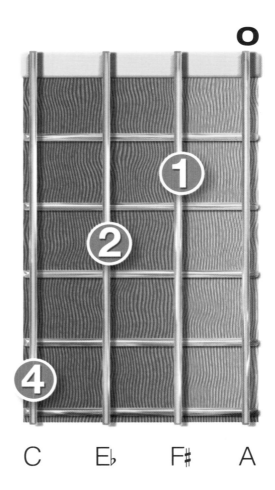

O

① ② ④

C   Eb   F#   A

F#/Gb

Chord Spelling
1st (F#), b3rd (A), b5th (C), bb7th (Eb)

F♯/G♭add9
Major add 9th

G♯   C♯   F♯   A♯

Chord Spelling
1st (F♯), 3rd (A♯), 5th (C♯), 9th (G♯)

F♯/G♭

G
Major

O

G   D   G   B

Chord Spelling
1st (G), 3rd (B), 5th (D)

A

A#/B♭

B

C

C#/D♭

D

D#/E♭

E

F

F#/G♭

G

G#/A♭

Gm
Minor

O

G   D   G   B♭

Chord Spelling
1st (G), ♭3rd (B♭), 5th (D)

G+
Augmented Triad

O

G   D#   G   B

Chord Spelling
1st (G), 3rd (B), #5th (D#)

G°
Diminished Triad

G   D♭   G   B♭

Chord Spelling
1st (G), ♭3rd (B♭), ♭5th (D♭)

G

Gsus2

Suspended 2nd

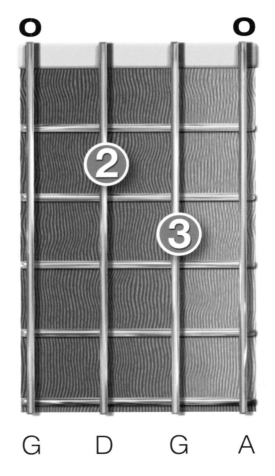

G D G A

Chord Spelling
1st (G), 2nd (A), 5th (D)

Gsus4
Suspended 4th

O

G   D   G   C

Chord Spelling
1st (G), 4th (C), 5th (D)

FREE ACCESS on smartphones
including iPhone & Android

Using any free QR code app,
scan and **HEAR** the chord

A

A♯/B♭

B

C

C♯/D♭

D

D♯/E♭

E

F

F♯/G♭

G

G6
Major 6th

Chord Spelling
1st (G), 3rd (B), 5th (D), 6th (E)

Gm6
Minor 6th

G   D   E   B♭

Chord Spelling
1st (G), ♭3rd (B♭), 5th (D), 6th (E)

G

Gmaj7
Major 7th

O

G   D   F#   B

Chord Spelling
1st (G), 3rd (B), 5th (D), 7th (F#)

G7

Dominant 7th

G   D   F   B

Chord Spelling

1st (G), 3rd (B), 5th (D), ♭7th (F)

A

A♭/B♭

B

C

C♯/D♭

D

E♭/E♭

E

F

G♭/G♭

G

G♯/A♭

G7sus4
Dominant 7th
Suspended 4th

G   D   F   C

Chord Spelling
1st (G), 4th (C), 5th (D), ♭7th (F)

Gm7
Minor 7th

O

G   D   F   B♭

Chord Spelling
1st (G), ♭3rd (B♭), 5th (D), ♭7th (F)

G

G°7
Diminished 7th

G   D♭   F♭   B♭

Chord Spelling
1st (G), ♭3rd (B♭), ♭5th (D♭), ♭♭7th (F♭)

Gadd9
Major add 9th

A   D   G   B

Chord Spelling
1st (G), 3rd (B), 5th (D), 9th (A)

G

G♯/A♭
Major

A♭   E♭   A♭   C

Chord Spelling
1st (A♭), 3rd (C), 5th (E♭)

G♯/A♭

G#/A♭m
Minor

A♭   E♭   A♭   C♭

Chord Spelling
1st (A♭), ♭3rd (C♭), 5th (E♭)

G#/A♭

G♯/A♭+
Augmented Triad

A♭   E   A♭   C

Chord Spelling
1st (A♭), 3rd (C), ♯5th (E)

A
A♯/B♭
B
C
C♯/D♭
D
D♯/E♭
E
F
F♯/G♭
G
G♯/A♭

G♯/A♭°
Diminished Triad

A♭   E♭♭   A♭   C♭

Chord Spelling
1st (A♭), ♭3rd (C♭), ♭5th (E♭♭)

G#/A♭sus2
Suspended 2nd

A♭   E♭   A♭   B♭

Chord Spelling
1st (A♭), 2nd (B♭), 5th (E♭)

A
A#/B♭
B
C
C#/D♭
D
D#/E♭
E
F
F#/G♭
G
G#/A♭

G#/A♭sus4
Suspended 4th

A♭   E♭   A♭   D♭

Chord Spelling
1st (A♭), 4th (D♭), 5th (E♭)

G♯/A♭6
Major 6th

A♭   E♭   F   C

Chord Spelling
1st (A♭), 3rd (C), 5th (E♭), 6th (F)

G♯/A♭m6
Minor 6th

| A♭ | E♭ | F | C♭ |

Chord Spelling
1st (A♭), ♭3rd (C♭), 5th (E♭), 6th (F)

G♯/A♭

G♯/A♭maj7
Major 7th

A♭   E♭   G   C

Chord Spelling
1st (A♭), 3rd (C), 5th (E♭), 7th (G)

G♯/A♭

G♯/A♭7
Dominant 7th

| A♭ | E♭ | G♭ | C |

Chord Spelling
1st (A♭), 3rd (C), 5th (E♭), ♭7th (G♭)

G#/A♭7sus4
Dominant 7th
Suspended 4th

A♭   E♭   G♭   D♭

Chord Spelling
1st (A♭), 4th (D♭), 5th (E♭), 7th (G♭)

G#/A♭m7
Minor 7th

A♭   E♭   G♭   C♭

Chord Spelling
1st (A♭), ♭3rd (C♭), 5th (E♭), ♭7th (G♭)

G#/A♭

G♯/A♭°7
Diminished 7th

A♭   E♭♭   G♭♭   C♭

Chord Spelling
1st (A♭), ♭3rd (C♭), ♭5th (E♭♭), ♭♭7th (G♭♭)

A
A♯/B♭
B
C
C♯/D♭
D
D♯/E♭
E
F
F♯/G♭
G
G♯/A♭

G♯/A♭add9
Major add 9th

| B♭ | E♭ | A♭ | C |

Chord Spelling
1st (A♭), 3rd (C), 5th (E♭), 9th (B♭)

flametreemusic.com

The Flame Tree Music website complements our range of print books and offers easy access to chords and scales online, and on the move, through tablets, smartphones, and desktop computers.

1. The site offers access to chord diagrams and finger positions for the guitar, piano/keyboard and ukulele, presenting a wide range of sound options to help develop good listening technique, and to assist you in identifying the chord and each note within it.

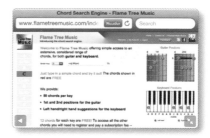

2. The site offers 12 **free** chords, those most commonly used in bands and songwriting.

3. A subscription is available if you'd like the full range of chords, **50** for **each key**.

4. Guitar chords are shown with **first** and **second positions on the fretboard**.

5. For the keyboard, you can **see** and **hear** each note in **left-** and **right-hand positions**.

6. Choose the key, then the chord name from the drop down menu. Note that the **red chords** are available **free**. Those in blue can be accessed with a subscription.

7. Once you've selected the chord, press **GO** and the details of the chord will be shown, with chord spellings, keyboard and guitar fingerings.

8. Sounds are provided in four easy-to-understand configurations.

9. flametreemusic.com also gives you access to **20 scales for each key**.